Legends of the West: The Life and Legacy of Doc Holliday

By Charles River Editors

About Charles River Editors

Charles River Editors was founded by Harvard and MIT alumni to provide superior editing and original writing services, with the expertise to create digital content for publishers across a vast range of subject matter. In addition to providing original digital content for third party publishers, Charles River Editors republishes civilization's greatest literary works, bringing them to a new generation via ebooks.

Visit charlesrivereditors.com for more information.

Introduction

John Henry "Doc" Holliday (1851-1887)

"Doc was a dentist, not a lawman or an assassin, whom necessity had made a gambler; a gentleman whom disease had made a frontier vagabond; a philosopher whom life had made a caustic wit; a long lean ash-blond fellow nearly dead with consumption, and at the same time the most skillful gambler and the nerviest, speediest, deadliest man with a six-gun that I ever knew."
– Wyatt Earp

Space may be the final frontier, but no frontier has ever captured the American imagination like the "Wild West", which still evokes images of dusty cowboys, outlaws, gunfights, gamblers, and barroom brawls over 100 years after the West was settled. A constant fixture in American pop culture, the 19th century American West continues to be vividly and colorful portrayed not just as a place but as a state of mind. In Charles River Editors' Legends of the West series, readers can get caught up to speed on the lives of America's most famous frontier figures in the time it takes to finish a commute, while learning interesting facts long forgotten or never known.

Of all the colorful characters that inhabited the West during the 19th century, the man who has earned an enduring legacy as the region's quirkiest is John Henry "Doc" Holliday (1851-1887), a dentist turned professional gambler who was widely recognized as one of the fastest draws in the West. In fact, the only thing that might have been faster than the deadly gunman's draw was his violent temper, which was easily set off when Holliday was drunk. By the early 1880s, Holliday had been arrested nearly 20 times.

That said, there were plenty of men in the West who gambled, drank, and dueled, and Holliday may have been lumped in with those whose names were forgotten but for his association with Wyatt Earp. It was this friendship that led to Holliday's role in the West's most famous shootout, the Gunfight at the O.K. Corrall, as well as the Earp Vendetta Ride. For those two events alone, Holliday's legacy has endured, and his unique characteristics have added a mystique, legendary quality to it.

Next to Earp, Holliday might be the second most recognizable name among the legends of the West, and yet several details of his life remain sketchy. *Legends of the West: The Life and Legacy of Doc Holliday* chronicles Holliday's life, while also analyzing his legacy and the mythology that has enveloped his story. Along with pictures of important people, places, and events in his life, you will learn about Doc Holliday like you never have before, in no time at all.

J.H. (Doc.) Holliday, as he appeared in the early eighties.

A photo believed to be of Doc Holliday in Tombstone in the early 1880s

Chapter 1: Holliday's Early Years

When John Henry Holliday was born on August 14, 1851, in Spalding County, Georgia, the Southern Frontier was less than two decades removed from being the land of the Cherokees. His father, Henry Burroughs Holliday, was a self-made man who believed in the Southern codes of honor, independence, and community. As a reward for assisting the First Georgia volunteers in removing the Cherokees and starting them on their Trail of Tears west, Henry Holliday was given 160 acres of land in Pike County.

Henry settled in the town of Griffin, which would later be part of the newly created Spalding County. For a man seeking a life of respectability, he could have not chosen a better wife than Alice Jane McKey of the South Carolina McKeys. Beautiful, fair-haired, and a lover of music, Alice became Henry's wife on January 8, 1849, three months before her 20th birthday. By the time Alice and Henry were expecting their first child, Henry was a respected man in the community, working as a druggist and accumulating land on the side. Martha Eleanora was born on December 3, 1849, but the baby was frail from the start and died half a year later on June 12, 1850.

When John Henry was born a little over a year later, Henry and Alice's grief turned to joy. Not even his cleft palate, which was surgically repaired in a delicate procedure for the times, could dampen their spirits. Their first-born son was a symbol of hope for the future. Henry and Alice never had more children, but their household was often full of extended relatives and even orphans that Henry agreed to care for.

Everything seemed to be falling into place until 1861, when it all changed in the South. Major Holliday joined the Confederate army on October 31, 1861, serving under General P.G.T. Beauregard. In the major's absence, John Henry grew closer to his mother. Alice was determined that her son would be a Southern gentleman, and indeed it was a quality that stayed with him for the rest of his life. When she became sick, John Henry's feelings of protectiveness for his mother only increased.

General Beauregard

In the mid-19th century, tuberculosis was called consumption, a play on the fact that it seemed to eat away at the body until its victims literally drowned when their lungs could no longer function. It was not believed to be contagious, but rather hereditary, and the treatment prescribed to women was usually to stay home and perform their typical domestic duties, which essentially amounted to doing nothing different than perhaps eating a more bland diet. When the major returned to a war-torn Georgia after resigning his commission due to chronic diarrhea, Alice was weak and bedridden. He felt like he had no choice but to move his family as far from the war front as he could while still remaining in Georgia. Thus, in 1864, he moved them to Valdosta.

Once the Holliday family arrived in their new home, John Henry attended the Valdosta Institute for grammar school, receiving rigorous training in rhetoric and the classics from Samuel Varnedoe, a man credited with focusing more on achievement and nurturing of learning than disciplining with a switch. John Henry was a good student, well mannered, and popular with his classmates, and at home he was developing a close relationship with his older cousin, Mattie, whose family had come to Valdosta to join his own. His relationship with Mattie is just one of the great mysteries of his life. Some suggest that their relationship turned to romance, although there was never any confirmation of this. Either way, they did keep in contact throughout his life and he wrote to Mattie often. However, his world was turned upside down when his mother died from consumption on September 16, 1866.

John Henry was furious when 23 year-old neighbor Rachel Martin married his father three months later. To him, as well as to other members of the family, it was disrespectful to his mother's memory, and it was only made worse when Major Holliday moved his family from their farm to a house owned by his new in-laws. Others questioned the circumstances that would call for such a quick marriage. With a lawsuit filed against him by his former brother-in-law, who wanted his deceased sister's property back and questioned Henry's fidelity, Major Holliday's once close-knit family started to unravel.

Congressional candidate J.W. Clift visited the county courthouse to make a campaign speech on April 4, 1868. The courthouse happened to also be the headquarters for the Freedmen's Bureau, which was created in 1865 to assist former slaves with emergency food, shelter, medical care, and in some cases, family reunification. Major Holliday's appointment as an agent for the Freedmen's Bureau upset local citizens, as well as his son. When a small explosion went off during Clift's speech, John Henry was one of the young men suspected of involvement. Whether the young Holliday was actually involved is not known for sure, but it is known that Major Holliday's son was becoming angry and rebellious enough to do it.

Chapter 2: John Henry Holliday, D.D.S.

Exactly why John Henry entered dental school is not clear, but chances are that he received some encouragement from his uncle, John Stiles Holliday, a respected physician who was living in Atlanta in 1869. Dr. Holliday was growing disillusioned with medicine and believed that dentistry was more respectable and, in many ways, more progressive. Dentists were already using anesthesia, while most doctors were still skeptical. Licensing standards for doctors were also loose, opening the door for scam artists selling questionable remedies. When Dr. Lucian Frink, a friend of Major Holliday's, agreed to be his preceptor, John Henry paid the $100 tuition and enrolled in Frink's alma mater, the Pennsylvania College of Dental Surgery.

Starting in October 1870, Holliday attended classes six days a week. The Valdosta Institute had prepared him well for the rigors of dental school. Chartered in 1856, the Pennsylvania College of Dental Surgery was one of the largest and most prestigious dental colleges in the world at the time, and in addition to attending lectures on topics such as chemistry, anatomy, and dental pathology, Holliday worked at the school's free clinic, which had developed an outstanding reputation for its dental care.

Holliday had never left Georgia before and, no doubt, Philadelphia was a new world for a young man who had been born and bred in the South. Holliday obviously went on to spend much of his life as a drinker and a gambler, and it would not be out of the realm of possibilities that he got his first exposure to these elements in Philadelphia. Still, Holliday was a good student. In March 1871, he returned to Valdosta to continue his training under Frink before going back to Philadelphia in September to complete his second year of studies. After writing his master's thesis, "Diseases of the Teeth," Holliday and 25 of his classmates attended graduation ceremonies and received their Doctor of Dental Surgery degrees.

It would be another five months before Holliday would receive his license to practice dentistry, because Georgia state law required that he be 21 years old and he was still only 20. In the meantime, he worked as an assistant to one of his classmates, A. Jameson Fuches, Jr., who opened a practice in St. Louis, Missouri.

The raucous river city offered Holliday more than professional experience. St. Louis was the home of a foster care runaway whose given name was Mary Katharine Harony. Born in Hungary, she had come to the U.S. and went by the name Kate Fisher, but in Western lore, she became best known by her nickname Big Nose Kate. Like many women of her time who had no family, she became a prostitute, and in 1872 she was living in a brothel and worked at a saloon not far from Dr. Fuches's office on Fourth Street.

Big Nose Kate (left) in 1865

Whether she started out as his girlfriend or he initially paid for her company, Kate and John Henry began their often-stormy relationship in St. Louis. Perhaps he was attracted to her courage, but her distrust of other people, especially of Wyatt Earp, would be a source of conflict in their relationship throughout much of Holliday's life. There is no evidence to support Kate's claim that they were married in Valdosta in 1876, but it is a fact that even though Holliday left St Louis without her in July 1872, it was far from the end of his time with Fisher.

Big Nose Kate, circa 1890

Holliday returned to Georgia just before his 21st birthday to claim the inheritance from his mother and then moved in with John Stiles Holliday in Atlanta, who by now had given up his medical practice for the grocery business. He renewed his friendship with his cousin, Robert, or Hub as he was known in the family, and the two handsome bachelors quickly established themselves in the Atlanta social scene. Hub would go on to become an esteemed dentist, graduating from the same school as John Henry, and he later helped found a dental college in Atlanta that was incorporated into Emory University in 1944.

John Stiles Holliday helped introduce his nephew to friends and associates in Atlanta with a party in the ballroom of his home and gave him a revolver just like the one he had given his three sons, an 1851 Colt revolver. The Holliday household in Atlanta also included Sophie Walton, the family's biracial servant. An expert card player who was adept with numbers, Sophie helped John Henry in his education as a gambler, providing information that would prove useful in the years that he would spend as a player and a dealer in the game of choice, faro. In the 19th century, Faro became one of the most popular gambling games in the U.S., especially in the West, where it was often called "Bucking the Tiger" because of the backs of early cards that featured a drawing of a Bengal Tiger.

Samuel Hape was also living with the Hollidays at that time. He had founded Atlanta Dental in 1868, and during the Civil War Hape was the only source of dental supplies for the Confederacy. He was acquainted with the dentist Arthur C. Ford and arranged for John Henry to have an interview with Dr. Ford. On July 26, 1872, Ford took out a notice in *The Atlanta Constitution* saying that Dr. John Holliday would be covering for him during his absence at a conference in August. Since Dr. Ford frequently had to travel, John Henry filled in for him on a regular basis.

Soon, John Henry became a landowner, assuming ownership of a building in Griffin that had belonged to his mother's family. When Hub had decided to quit dental school, thinking it was no longer necessary, John Henry talked him out of it and agreed to be Hub's preceptor at his alma mater. John Stiles promised financial assistance for the two young men to set up their practice together. Everything was aligning for John Henry Holliday to be a dentist and a respected member of Atlanta society.

Chapter 3: Doc Holliday Heads West

Texas

Dr. Arthur Ford was not a well man. Like Holliday's mother, Dr. Ford was also suffering from consumption, and by New Year's Day 1873, Ford announced that he was going to Florida to recuperate. He turned his practice over to Dr. J. Cooper, not Holliday. Holliday had endured a difficult Christmas. His uncle (Mattie's father), Robert Holliday, died on Christmas Eve, and John Henry was with his family at the funeral. Weeks later, Francisco E'Dalgo, a Mexican orphan that lived with John Henry as a child, died from consumption. The next day, Holliday sold his half of the building he inherited from his mother in Griffin, pocketing $1,800. By the summer, he was in Dallas, Texas.

Why Holliday left Georgia for Dallas is another mystery and subject to much speculation. The most common theory is that he went west for his health. Bouts of coughing that got progressively worse into the winter of 1872 led to confirmation that Holliday, too, had consumption. There was no cure, nor was there really an effective treatment. Some said that Holliday was told to go west where the air is drier and, presumably, easier on his lungs. If there is a flaw to this theory, it is that Dallas can be quite humid and the weather is not that much different from Atlanta. If Holliday truly wanted to seek out dry air, he could have proceeded directly to the desert of the Southwest.

Another theory for his departure is that he was in love with his cousin, Mattie. It was not unheard of for first cousins to marry at the time, but Mattie was Catholic and her religion did not permit it. Certainly, they had a special relationship, but nobody would confirm that their relationship had ever turned to romance. Mattie burned some of the letters he wrote to her and another family member burned the rest of them years later. When he began to transform from Dr. Holliday, the dentist, into Doc Holliday, the gunman, he still wrote to her even though by that time she was a nun.

A third theory, repeated by lawman turned journalist Bat Masterson, is that Holliday had committed murder and was forced to leave town. Few people deny that Holliday was involved in a shooting incident at swimming hole on the Withlacooche River near Valdosta. His uncle Tom McKey owned land near the river, and members of the family claimed a nearby swimming hole as their own. The African Americans who swam there had been advised to swim elsewhere. One day, a group of white men that included Holliday saw some young African Americans swimming there, despite previous warnings. Some say Holliday drew his Colt and shot over their heads, while others say he killed one, possibly three people. According to Masterson, Holliday said that his family advised him to go away for a while and helped him get to Dallas. Like other similar stories about Holliday, there is no documented evidence or record of the shooting, but that was not at all unusual for this period of history either. White violence against African Americans routinely occurred and went unreported, and it is also not unlikely that family members would sanitize the story, just as they might burn incriminating letters.

Whatever the cause, and perhaps it was a combination of all three theories, John Henry Holliday left his home state and headed west.

Bat Masterson

The Emergence of a Dangerous Reputation

Dallas was not simply a random location to Holliday. He was acquainted with another dentist, Dr. John A. Seeger and became his partner in his practice in the summer of 1873. Seeger, a non-drinker, was probably pleased if Holliday's claim that he not only stopped drinking but also joined the local temperance society was true. Business was good for the young dentists, but once again, the partnership did not last long and ended the following March. Holliday's taste for whiskey and gambling had resurfaced, as did his illness. Indeed, the correlation between the desire for alcohol and the increasing coughing fits may have gone hand-in-hand.

Holliday was arrested in April 1874 for operating a keno game, but since he paid his property taxes on June 1, it appeared that he was still going to try and stay in Dallas. However, he left for Denison, an edgier, rougher town than Dallas, before the month was over, and it can be safely assumed that dentistry was taking a backseat to the allure of the gaming tables by now. Of course, Holliday may have been left with little choice; it is difficult to imagine that many people wanted a dentist with a persistent cough to treat them.

Regardless of how and why Holliday came to Denison, Holliday was starting to develop a reputation as a dangerous man, though the fact that so many of the stories about him are not supported by witnesses or documentation raises some questions. Certainly, it is not unusual if crimes in a more lawless time go unreported or if records were lost, but some historians have begun to question if Holliday spread the rumors about himself. The reasons may have simply been rooted in self-protection for a man, typically carrying a lot of cash, who often traveled alone through treacherous territory. Others believed that Holliday simply felt that he had little to lose because he knew he would not have a long life, even though he did look for treatment for his condition more than once.

Between 1875 and 1877, Holliday roamed across the West, and wherever he went, stories about shootings and other mayhem followed him. Known now as "Doc," but perhaps using the alias of Tom McKey, there were reports of him killing a solider in Jacksboro, Texas and cutting a man's face in Denver, Colorado. Some say he joined the goldrush in Deadwood, South Dakota, while still other reports placed him in Cheyenne, Wyoming before heading back to Texas. Wyatt Earp claims that Holliday was in Fort Griffin, Texas with Kate Fisher in 1877. Earp was there because he was on the trail of a band of outlaws known as The Trio. He never caught up with them – Bat Masterson eventually arrested them in Kansas in 1878 – but Earp did strike up a friendship with Holliday that became part of both men's legends.

Wyatt Earp

Wyatt and Doc

To a great extent, the lives of Doc Holliday and Wyatt Earp will forever be defined by a 30-second gun battle in Tombstone, Arizona, which Earp would spend his final years trying to forget. Holliday was there, too, even though Earp told him he didn't need to be. In fact, no stories about Earp in Tombstone are complete without Holliday. However, Holliday has come to be viewed by many as Earp's sidekick, which is not accurate. Masterson wrote of Holliday in "Human Life" magazine in 1907, "His whole heart and soul were wrapped up in Wyatt Earp…"[1] Holliday was a good friend to Earp and raised to be loyal to his friends, but he was nobody's sidekick.

They met in a saloon in Fort Griffin, but their friendship took hold in Dodge City, Kansas. Upon leaving Texas, Holliday wrote to Mattie in 1878 that he had "enjoyed as much of this as [I] could stand."[2] Earp, as tall as Holliday but much more physically intimidating, aspired to make some cash more than he aspired to be a lawman. Still, he was respected as deputy marshal of Dodge City, which needed a man like Earp to help keep order when the Texas cowboys were in town to blow off steam.

By 1876, Dodge City, Kansas had become a popular destination spot for cattle drives starting from as far south as Texas, and though it's known that Wyatt was appointed an assistant Marshal in Dodge City, but it's unclear how much time he spent there. It has been widely theorized that Earp even spent some time in the legendary frontier boomtown of Deadwood in the Black Hills of South Dakota, which is as popular as ever today thanks to the shooting of Wild Bill Hicock and a critically acclaimed HBO show about the town. It's also known that Wyatt spent some time in 1877 gambling down in Texas, which is where he first met Holliday.

Masterson was the sheriff when Holliday arrived and claimed to tolerate Holliday and his stories more out of respect for Earp than for any good feelings about Doc. Masterson thought that Holliday was dangerous and perhaps a little crazy. When Masterson became a writer, he wrote about Holliday, "He was selfish and had a perverse nature – traits not calculated to make a man popular in the early days of the frontier."[3]

Clearly, Holliday's reputation had preceded him before he arrived in Dodge City, and according to Earp, Holliday's departure from Fort Griffin was hastened by an incident at a poker game involving a man named Ed Bailey. Holliday reportedly advised Bailey to stop playing with the pile of discarded cards, called deadwood, and focus more on the game, which was a way of politely asking him to stop cheating. When Bailey continued to cheat, Holliday whipped out a knife that he always carried and stabbed the man. When Holliday took off to his room, Kate deliberately set a shed on fire to create a diversion and the two escaped to Kansas. Whether the incident really happened the way Earp, who was not a witness, told it or whether it even happened in Texas, nobody knows, but it did contribute to Holliday's reputation as a man who would kill you before he backed down.

---

[1] "Bat Masterson Not Impressed by Doc Holliday." *Territorial News.* December 15, 2010.
[2] Gary L. Roberts. *Doc Holliday: The Life and Legend.* Page 89.
[3] *Territorial News*

Earp also claimed that it was this streak in Holliday that saved Earp's life in 1878 and cemented their friendship. Earp said that he found himself surrounded by outlaws somewhere near the Long Branch Saloon on Dodge City's famous Front Street. Holliday was nearby at a gaming table and saw the men closing in on Earp. After asking the card dealer if he could borrow his six-shooter, Holliday bolted for the door, drew both his own gun and the borrowed gun, and ordered the outlaws to put up their hands. Earp said this gave him time to draw his own gun and place the men under arrest.

Las Vegas, New Mexico

Initially, at least, Holliday felt a sense of acceptance in Dodge City that eluded him in Texas. Certainly the environment in the dusty cowtown suited him, with enough saloons and faro tables to keep him entertained. The very existence of Dodge City, located in western Kansas, was tied to the state Holliday had left behind. Wealthy cattle barons from Texas passed through and, in many cases, left both their cattle and their cash in Dodge City. The more saloons, brothels, and gaming tables there were, the more opportunity there was for the businessmen of Dodge City to make a profit.

One thing that Dodge City did not have when Holliday arrived was a dentist, prompting him to take out an advertisement in *The Dodge City Times* on June 8, 1878. He offered his dentistry services to the community, with a money-back guarantee. His office was located in Room 24 at the Dodge House Hotel, adjacent to a billiards hall. Holliday even had a pocket dental kit, complete with the basic dental tools of the day, and an inscription with his name and the address of his office. All of this suggests that Holliday might have considered settling down in Kansas.

As it turned out, Holliday did not settle down. He was more successful as a gambler than a dentist, and the dust of Dodge City did little to help his health. His cough was deep and persistent, while his voice had become hoarse due to ulcers in his throat, which often made it hard for him to speak above a whisper. He lost more weight and his color alternated between red and pale. The humidity of Kansas was also no help, but there was word that the Montezuma Hot Springs in Gallinas Canyon in New Mexico had helped others suffering from consumption.

The timing was right to move on if Holliday desired to do so. Dodge City's prime cattle running season was coming to an end with winter just around the corner. The town was also trying to get a handle on prostitution and gambling, and on August 6, 1878 it passed ordinances outlawing both. They were not truly outlawed as the town wanted to regulate the big moneymakers, not eliminate them, but the result was making it more expensive and difficult for a man like Holliday to gamble. Holliday also claimed to be falsely implicated in a robbery at a local store, so with these factors in mind, he and Kate moved on to Las Vegas, New Mexico in the winter of 1878.

They made it as far as Trinidad, Colorado when the snow began to fall. With Doc's health failing, the faced a difficult decision. They either stayed in brutally cold Trinidad or risked Holliday deteriorating even more on the road. Ultimately, they hired a teamster who was on his way to Santa Fe to transport Kate and a very ill Doc to Las Vegas by rail. Doc and Kate arrived in Las Vegas just before Christmas 1878, referring to themselves as Dr. and Mrs. J.H. Holliday. It may have been simply easier to explain their relationship this way even if Kate was just his common-law wife. Northwest of the town plaza was the mecca for consumption patients, 22 springs at the base of the mountains that produced water ranging in temperatures from 110 degrees up to 140 degrees. Las Vegas was full of people, most young and mostly wealthy, who had come to these springs, hoping for a cure for their consumption. They called themselves the Lungers Club.

After settling in, Holliday opened a dental practice in an office not far from the town plaza. He shared space with jeweler and watchmaker, William Leonard, another young man afflicted with consumption. Holliday, already well-acquainted with men with questionable pasts, was not put off by the story that Leonard shot Jose Mares the previous fall in front of a local store and then took a beating from Mares' friends. They developed a friendship that lasted until Leonard was indicted on charges and left town.

Holliday began to recover his strength in Las Vegas and soon felt well enough to open a saloon. However, neither the record-breaking frigid temperatures nor the new law that would prohibit gambling within New Mexico Territory would help Holliday's income as dentist or a saloonkeeper/gambler. He was fined $25 for running a monte table in March 1879, prompting him to head back to Dodge City, this time without Kate. Holliday made a little money there helping Masterson organize a group of fighters for the Atchison, Topeka, & Santa Fe Railroad. The railroad had asked Sheriff Masterson to help fight off attacks on workers in a contested pass at Canon City, Colorado. Holliday did a bit more work for the railroad before he went back to Las Vegas.

By this time, Las Vegas was preparing for the arrival of the railroad, which ultimately bypassed the town by about a mile. Still, businesses were being built, plans were being made and many of the gamblers that Holliday knew from Dodge City followed the line into town. Trouble followed him, too. He was accused of shooting a man named Mike Gordon, who opened gunfire when one of the saloon girls turned down his advances. There were reports of other trouble, too, but like many of the tales about Holliday, it is not known if they ever occurred.

Holliday may have wanted to stay in Las Vegas, but he was soon on the road again. Wyatt Earp and his common-law wife, Mattie, had come to town, talking about a silver strike in Arizona. Wyatt's brother Virgil had been living in northern Arizona, serving in various law enforcement roles in the capital of Prescott, and when Virgil was appointed U.S. deputy marshal of Pima County in southern Arizona, he sent for his brothers, Wyatt and Morgan, to serve as special deputies to help him deal with the cowboys. With the lure of striking it rich in the silver mines, Wyatt Earp and Mattie Blaylock left Kansas in 1879 for the silver-mining boomtown of Tombstone, Arizona.

Virgil Earp

After a stop in Albuquerque, Holliday headed west again, this time for Arizona.

Chapter 4: Becoming a Legend in Arizona

Prescott

Prescott, Arizona bore little resemblance to Tombstone. The northern Arizona town was the capital, lost the title to Tucson in 1867, then got it back again in 1877 before losing it for good to Phoenix in 1889. As the capital city, it was busy and had its share of gambling halls and saloons along famed Whiskey Row. However, it was not a boomtown and lacked the edginess of Tombstone.

In 1877, Ed Schieffelin was working for the U.S. government as an Indian scout in Arizona. After leaving the Grand Canyon area, Schieffelin moved south and was stationed at Fort Huachuca, not far from the Mexican border. As he was known to do, Schieffelin went out on his own to search for "rocks." Other soldiers in the camp told him that the only stone he would find out in the rugged hills was his tombstone. When he found silver, the soon-to-be millionaire named his first mine "The Tombstone."

Schieffelin

As word of Schieffelin's discovery spread, prospectors streamed into the camp near where he had staked his claim. The tents soon gave way to buildings, and when the national census was taken in 1880, Tombstone had 2,100 residents. By the time a special census was taken in Arizona in 1882 to accounting for the new counties that had sprung up in the past two years, Tombstone reported 5,300 residents, second only to Tucson. At its peak, as many as 15,000 people crowded Tombstone's dusty streets.

Tombstone in 1881

Earp had invited Holliday to join him in Tombstone, which stayed in Holliday's mind as he gambled and walked the streets of Prescott. They had arrived in Prescott together in November 1879 and immediately went to see Virgil and Allie Earp, who had been Prescott residents for two years when they told Wyatt about the silver strike. When Jim, Virgil, and Wyatt Earp and their families were ready to go to Tombstone about a week later, where they planned to meet their brother, Morgan, Holliday had already found the gambling scene in Prescott to his liking. He was on a hot streak, so he and Kate opted to stay. This suited Kate just fine as she never really liked Wyatt and did not want Doc to be around him, either.

James Earp

Kate and Doc's relationship was littered with turbulent periods resulting in frequent separations. One of those periods appears to have come at some point in their stay in Prescott because the 1880 census listed Holliday as a single man. One of his roommates at the boarding house where he lived was John J. Gosper, who happened to be the acting governor of Arizona in General John C. Fremont's absence. No doubt Holliday and Gosper had interesting discussions on the point of alcohol, considering that Gosper was an active member of the temperance society and Holliday was an active indulger of whiskey. Soon, though, Holliday would be on the move again.

Tombstone

Whether it was due to the end of his hot streak at the tables or due to strong recruitment effort by Wyatt, it was September 1880 when Holliday finally arrived in Tombstone, according to voter registration records. Kate, irritated at Doc for reuniting with the Earps, went to Globe, Arizona instead.

Few, if any, people paid attention to the wagon that carried Earp and Mattie into town in December 1879. Only a few hundred people lived there at the time the Earp family arrived to join Virgil, but the signs of growing wealth were there. Soon there would be churches, restaurants, and shops, some of which were even indicative of the sophistication of the Victorian Era. These symbols of the times often stood in stark contrast to the dusty mines nearby. The Earps had come to Tombstone to cash in like everybody else, but even at this time, Tombstone was quickly becoming the domain of more sophisticated mining companies from cities such as

New York, San Francisco, or London. Little was left to small, individual prospectors, even as the town's population exploded over the next several years, and any hopes of getting rich off of the silver mines were short-lived.

When Holliday arrived, Tombstone was still rough around the edges, but it was still also quite a bit different than the town that the Earps rolled into the previous December. Prospector tents from miners looking for the motherlode had given way to permanent buildings and the census shot up from a few hundred when the Earps arrived to 2,100 in 1880. A special census in Arizona in 1882, made necessary by the new counties that were created over the previous two years, indicated that Tombstone's population had grown to 5,300. At one point, it would swell to 15,000 people.

It did not take long for the town to be invaded by wealthy businessmen and entrepreneurs. Their wives could be seen dressed in their finest Victorian dresses, walking along the dusty sidewalks or playing lawn tennis at posh hotels that butted up against the town's dirty mines. Any hopes of individual prospectors, such as the Earps, cashing in were quickly dashed when larger, better financed mining companies from the likes of New York and San Francisco moved into town to strip the mountains of their silver.

Businessmen weren't the only ones making their way to Tombstone. Though cowboys have been historically associated with courage and heroism, to call someone a cowboy at this time was an insult. Ranching and herding were legitimate professions, but a cowboy was a thief. Given its proximity to the border, Tombstone attracted its share of cowboys, who went into Mexico to steal cattle (often murdering innocent Mexicans in the process) and then brought the cattle to Tombstone to sell them to legitimate ranchers. This did not sit well with the businesses that owned the mines. The corporate - and largely Republican - establishment that had come to Tombstone to make money wanted the Earps to keep order. Arizona was still a territory and could not expect to achieve statehood, nor could the corporations expect to attract investors, if chaos and lawlessness reigned. Thus, despite hoping to leave law enforcement behind, Wyatt soon found himself needing work, and by the summer of 1880, he was deputy sheriff in Tombstone.

The Oriental Saloon

The Oriental Saloon was not only the most luxurious saloon and gambling hall in Tombstone, it was one of the finest in the entire West, making it a natural place for Holliday to frequent. On July 22, 1880, The Tombstone Daily Epitaph reported about the Saloon:

> "Last evening the portals were thrown open and the public permitted to gaze upon the most elegantly furnished saloon this side of the Golden Gate. Twenty-eight burners suspended in neat chandeliers afforded an illumination of ample brilliancy and the bright rays reflected from the many colored crystals in the bar sparkled like a December icing in the sunshine. The saloon comprises two apartments. To the right of the main entrance is the bar, beautifully carved, finished in white and gilt and capped with a handsomely polished top. In the rear of this stand a brace of sideboards....They were made for the Baldwin Hotel, of San Francisco....The back apartment is covered with a brilliant body brussels [sic] carpet and suitably furnished after the style of a grand club room, with conveniences for the wily dealers in polished ivory....Tombstone has taken the lead and [to] Messrs. Joyce and Co. our congratulations."

When Holliday arrived, the town was experiencing a gambling war between the so-called Easterners, gamblers who came from east of the Pacific Coast, and the Slopers, mostly from California. Wyatt had recently been given an interest in the Oriental's gambling hall, providing him with a cut of the concessions in exchange for helping keep order among the gamblers who hoped to disrupt the town's gambling arrangements.

One of the men doing the disrupting was John E. Tyler from Jackson County, Missouri. Tyler got into trouble in Tombstone on September 23, 1880 when he got into an argument with a gambler associated with the Easterners, but others jumped in and defused the situation before it got out of hand. On October 10, it was Holliday's turn to tussle with Tyler. The two men, unarmed due to the city ordinance against carrying a concealed weapon, got into an argument. Milton Joyce, who leased the bar and was the saloonkeeper that night, helped separate the two men and ordered them to leave. Tyler left, but Holliday began to argue with Joyce. With little effort, Joyce, a much larger man than Holliday, physically removed him from the bar and deposited him into the street.

Joyce

Holliday's pistol had been checked behind the bar and when he walked back into the Oriental to ask for it, Joyce refused. Undeterred, Holliday went to his room at Fly's boardinghouse, got another pistol and went back to the Oriental with his gun drawn. Joyce came out from behind the bar with a gun and may have shot it once, but definitely used it to give Holliday a beating, prompting many to think that Holliday was surely going to die. Shots were fired from all corners by this point and one hit Joyce in the hand. When it was obvious Doc's wounds were not critical, Holliday was arrested and paid a $30 fine. The incident was not over, though, and neither was the feud. The following May, he was indicted by the Grand Jury and after a continuance, a trial was scheduled for October 6, 1881. Holliday would never appear for the trial.

For a time after that, Holliday managed to stay out of legal trouble, focusing his interests on mining properties, acquiring water rights, and, of course, gambling. Kate visited him more than once to try to persuade him to return to Globe with her, where she had opened a hotel. Still harboring bad feelings for the Earps, she no doubt made her feelings known because on at least one occasion, their argument resulted in Doc getting arrested. Her attempts to separate Doc from the Earps only served to drive a wedge in her own relationship with him.

The Origins of the Feud with the Clantons and McLaurys

Even though he was technically a lawman, Wyatt Earp's taste for saloons and gaming tables caused people to talk. The Democratic ranchers saw Wyatt and Virgil as enforcers for the Republican businessmen who were in town to profit from the mines, while the Republicans were growing weary of the lawlessness in Tombstone. There would be no way that Arizona would attract investors, let alone be awarded statehood, if order was not restored.

The difficulties that the Earps ran into stemmed largely from conflict with the cowboys. These were not the cowboy heroes of the West, but rather they were thieves. Because of its location near the Mexican border, Tombstone was a strong lure for cowboys, who dipped down below the border to steal cattle, then brought them back north of the border to sell them. Federal law initially paid little attention to this and if the federal marshals did not care, it made the job that much more difficult for the Earps.

Not surprisingly, Wyatt quickly found himself caught up in adventure, and controversy, on the job. On October 28, 1880, Tombstone marshal Fred White headed to Allen Street to break up a group of intoxicated men shooting their guns into the air, apparently at the Moon. As White grabbed the pistol of an outlaw cowboy named Curly Bill Brocius, it went off, hitting White in the groin. Wyatt, seeing the start of the confrontation, commandeered someone's pistol and pistol-whipped Curly Bill, all while Curly Bill's friends started shooting at him. White died days later, and even though the Earps likely saved Curly Bill's life by taking him into custody before the mob got hold of him, he remained permanently bitter about being pistol-whipped, and he was implicated by at least one person in the murder of Morgan Earp in March 1882. Curly Bill had become Arizona's most famous outlaw after the shooting of White, but his reign would be short. Less than two years later, Curly Bill would die in a shootout at the hands of none other than Wyatt Earp.

Curly Bill

   Despite the controversy with Curly Bill, Wyatt had his sights set higher than deputy. He wanted to be the sheriff of Cochise County. News drifted down from Prescott in Spring 1881 that Tombstone would be named the seat of the new county and Earp, a Northerner with Republican ties, thought he had the inside track. However, Governor Fremont indicated that he planned to appoint Democrat Johnny Behan instead and Earp withdrew from consideration. This did not, however, change his feelings about his opponent. They were competing for more than the sheriff's office. They were competing for a woman. Mattie Blaylock was Earp's common-law wife when he arrived in Tombstone, but that did not stop him from having feelings for Josephine "Sadie" Marcus, who was living with Behan.

Behan

Sadie

The situation between Earp and Behan did not improve when a Wells Fargo stagecoach on its way to Tombstone from Benson, Arizona was robbed on March 15, 1881. The robbers got away with $26,000, and the driver and a passenger were murdered. Holliday's troubles with Milt Joyce, as well as his trouble with Kate, resurfaced when Kate went back to Tombstone in July. Once again, Kate and Doc argued and Kate turned to alcohol to console herself. Behan and Joyce came across Kate in her drunken condition and suggested a way for her to get back at it Holliday. She swore an affidavit saying that Doc had committed the robbery in Benson. She later said, "I became desperate and in a vain hope of breaking up their [the Earps] association with Doc, whom I loved…I had known I was taking a desperate chance, and I was not astonished when I lost out."[4]

Behan arrested Holliday on July 5, but the case was dropped on July 9. Not a shred of evidence existed to implicate Holliday, but the incident stayed in the minds of many. As for Kate, Doc sent her on her way back to Globe. Meanwhile, the actual killers had yet to be caught and Wells Fargo was unhappy. The company personally insured all cargo and needed to regain the trust of its customers. They wanted the bandits, dead or alive, and they wanted an example made of them. Sheriff Behan organized one posse and Virgil organized another, which included Holliday, Wyatt, and Masterson. Virgil Earp's posse tracked down a man who admitted to holding horses while the robbery occurred and they turned the man over to Behan. The man later escaped from jail, but the Earps claimed that Behan let him go.

---

[4] Reynolds, 155.

Wyatt Earp still had his mind set on getting the sheriff's office and thought that the stagecoach robbery could help, albeit indirectly. He worked out a deal with Ike Clanton, who was well acquainted with the cowboys that made their way in and out of Tombstone. Earp was confident that the cowboys knew who pulled off the robbery and if he could get enough information and solve the case, it seemed like he could score enough political points to become sheriff. Earp offered Clanton $6,000 for his help, which Clanton could not turn down. However, his only condition was that Earp keep the deal a secret. He knew if the cowboys found out about his betrayal, they would kill him. Wyatt later testified that he had also offered a reward to Frank McLaury for information about the identities of the cowboys, and Ike Clanton would later testify that Wyatt had admitted the Earps and Holliday were involved in the robbery themselves.

Clanton never got the chance to collect because the three cowboys that were responsible for the robbery and murder were killed in New Mexico after getting mixed up in a barroom brawl, but the secret between Earp and Clanton remained.

Ike Clanton

Harboring this secret did not ease Clanton's mind. He was convinced that Earp told Holliday about the arrangement, but Earp denied it. Clanton tried to goad Earp into admitting that he told Holliday by saying that Doc himself said he knew about the deal. Holliday was in Tucson when, on October 21, Wyatt sent Morgan to get him and ask him to return to Tombstone. Wyatt wanted to ask Holliday himself what, if anything, he knew. When Holliday arrived, he assured Wyatt he knew nothing about a deal between him and Ike Clanton, who had briefly left town to tend to other business.

Throughout the middle months of 1881, the resentment between the Earps and McLaurys also began to mount. When another stagecoach was robbed near Tombstone on September 8, it was determined that the robbers were Pete Spence and Frank Stilwell, both friends of the McLaury brothers. After they were arrested and released on bail, Virgil Earp arrested the pair again on October 13, either for a different charge or for a different robbery, but the McLaurys believed that Earp was harassing the two and arresting them for the same charge as before. Frank McLaury warned Morgan Earp that if the Earps arrested the McLaurys or their friends again, they were dead men.

Frank McLaury

On October 25, 1881, Clanton returned to Tombstone with Tom McLaury. The more he drank, the more his paranoia got the best of him. The more paranoid he got, the more he talked, and several people said they heard him make threats about killing Wyatt. When Holliday saw Clanton at the Alhambra Saloon, he directly confronted him and suggested that he stop saying that Earp had betrayed him. By now, Clanton was extremely drunk and continued his threats. Holliday responded by calling Clanton a liar. The incident was on the verge of escalating into a gunfight when Virgil intervened and threatened to arrest them both.

When Clanton saw Wyatt later in the evening, he told him he would get him in the morning. Wyatt ignored Clanton and went home to bed. Clanton, however, did not go to bed. He made his way to the Oriental for more drinking and a poker game with Behan, and, of all people, Virgil, who played cards that night with a pistol lying across his lap.

The Gunfight at the O.K. Corral

The O.K. Corral in 1882

When the Earps and Holliday woke up the next morning, October 26, 1882, they were told that Ike Clanton was walking the streets of Tombstone, going from saloon to saloon to announce his intentions to kill them. Some said Clanton went into the telegraph office to wire for help, and the town began to buzz with concern that a gang of angry cowboys was about to descend on Tombstone. Holliday could not help but hear the rumors and went to help. Earp told him, "This is none of your affair," to which Holliday said, "That is a hell of thing to say to me."[5] After the events that followed, many questioned why Holliday, known to have a quick temper, would be asked to help disarm the Clantons and the McLaurys, if that was Virgil Earp's intention.

In addition to Clanton's threats, Wyatt got into a physical confrontation with Tom McLaury, pistol-whipping him outside the courthouse after Tom had told him he was unarmed despite plainly and visibly carrying a revolver tucked near his right hip. It was for this reason that the Earps may have assumed Tom was armed when the gunfight started hours later.

No mob of angry cowboys ever appeared, but by the early afternoon, Ike Clanton had been joined by his brother Billy, cowboy Billy Claiborne, and Frank and Tom McLaury. The group of five were standing in a vacant lot on Fremont Street near the rear of the O.K. Corrall, in close proximity to where Holliday was renting a room and on the route to the homes of the Earps, possibly intending to serve a threatening warning to them. Around 2:30 p.m., Sheriff Behan attempted to persuade the cowboys to disarm themselves, but his request was quickly rejected.

---

[5] Roberts, 194.

The O.K. Corral is in yellow. The fighting took place in the green circle and alley

At about 3:00 p.m., Wyatt, Morgan, and Virgil Earp, along with Holliday, headed to the lot to confront the cowboys. The Earps were carrying revolvers, while Holliday had a pistol and a shotgun given to him by Virgil, which he had concealed under his long coat to avoid alarming the citizens of Tombstone.

Despite the fact that the most famous gunfight in American history took place moments later, exactly how it all went down remains heavily disputed and not completely clear. The Earps claimed that Virgil approached the Clantons and the McLaurys, stopping within a few feet of them to inform them that they were under arrest. Some say that Billy Clanton and Frank

McLaury were about to surrender, while the Earps claimed that the two went for their guns. One resident, Martha J. King, claimed the Earps told Holliday to "let them have it" and initiated the gunfight.

Who started the shooting was disputed, but everyone agreed that two shots were fired almost simultaneously, touching off the firing. However it started, the gunfight lasted, by all accounts, about 30 seconds. When it was over, an unarmed Ike Clanton and Billy Claiborne had run away, but the McLaury brothers, including an unarmed Tom, were dead in the street. Billy Clanton had suffered a painful and fatal gunshot wound to the chest, still slumping near the corner of the Macdonald house, where he had been leaning when the shooting started. Virgil and Morgan Earp were wounded, as was Holliday. It is believed that Billy Clanton and Frank McLaury, even after being wounded, continued shooting, and one of them hit Morgan Earp across the back. Virgil thought Billy Clanton hit him in the calf and began firing at him after being injured. Frank McLaury hit Holliday in a pocket and grazed him, incensing him and leading him to chase after Frank shouting, "That son of a bitch has shot me, and I am going to kill him." Wyatt managed to walk away without so much as a scratch. According to Big Nose Kate, when Holliday came back to his room he openly wept, stating, "That was awful—awful."

Tom McLaury

The initial reaction was that the Earps and Holliday were heroes. *The Tombstone Epitaph*'s described the shootout, "Wyatt Earp stood up and fired in rapid succession, as cool as a cucumber, and was not hit." The *San Francisco Examiner* suggested that Tombstone's residents be grateful to have the Earps on their side of the law. However, that sentiment did not last long. Many in Tombstone believed that the three dead men were murdered in cold blood, and they wondered why the Earps would ever ask a hothead like Doc Holliday to help them disarm the McLaurys and the Clantons. The local undertaker displayed the three corpses in their coffins in his window with a sign that read, "Murdered in the Streets of Tombstone."

The corpses of Tom McLaury, Frank McLaury, and Billy Clanton were publicly displayed in the undertaker's window.

Ike Clanton filed murder charges against Holliday and the Earps. Wyatt and Doc spent 16 days in jail, while Virgil Earp was temporarily suspended as town marshal. Just over a month after the shootout, the case was brought before Justice Wells Spicer. Ultimately, he found in favor of the defendants, determining that there was too little evidence to indict the defendants and that the evidence that did exist suggested they had acted within the law. Still, the ruling further incensed many people in Tombstone and left Ike Clanton still wanting revenge. The tension and assassination threats directed at the Earps were enough to lead the federal government to take notice, particularly because the cowboys continued to run amok unchecked in Mexico and the government wanted to avoid an international incident.

Targeting the Earps

It took little time for Clanton to get his revenge. On December 28, 1881, Virgil was ambushed in the street and shot in the arm by a shotgun blast as he left the Oriental Hotel. The shooter had hidden in drugstore that was under construction across the street. The force of the shot spun Virgil around and blew his arm into two, but he did not leave his feet until collapsing into Wyatt's arms back across the street. He would have no use of the arm for the rest of his life.

The shooter was never identified, but Ike Clanton's hat was found near where the shots had been fired. Clanton was later acquitted after several eyewitnesses testified he was not in Tombstone at the time of the shooting. In response to the attack on Virgil, Wyatt requested from the U.S. Marshal Crawley Dake that he be appointed a deputy U.S. marshal and given the ability to choose his own deputies, a request that was granted. The Earps racked up such expenses while bolstering their protection and swelling their ranks that Wyatt later had to mortgage his own house, and it was foreclosed on after he failed to repay the debt.

A few months after the attempt on Virgil's life, the Earp brothers' luck ran out. A few months later, in March 1882, Morgan Earp was playing pool in a billiards hall after attending a theater show. As he was playing, gunmen entered an alley outside the building and fired into the room, hitting Morgan in the spine. Wyatt was nearly hit by one of the bullets himself, which went straight over his head. As the gunmen escaped into the night, Morgan died within the hour.

Morgan Earp

Holliday and the Earp Vendetta Ride

Now it was the Earps and Holliday's turn to seek revenge. Two days after Morgan's death, which happened to be Wyatt's 34th birthday, the grieving Wyatt made arrangements for Morgan's body to be sent to their father's home in Colma, California. Morgan was reportedly buried in a suit that belonged to Holliday. Virgil and his wife, Allie, left for San Francisco under the watchful eye of armed guards, and Holliday joined Wyatt when it was time for Virgil and Allie to board the train from Tucson to San Francisco.

As the train left the station in Tucson, Wyatt claimed to have seen Ike Clanton and Frank Stilwell lying in wait for Virgil. After a brief chase, Clanton got away, but Wyatt shot and killed Stilwell, leaving his body riddled with bullets by the railroad tracks. Though it was just days after the attack on Morgan, Wyatt may already have believed that Stilwell was one of the men who shot at Morgan. Pete Spence's wife later claimed that Spence and Stilwell were among a group of men who had returned home shortly after Morgan had been shot, and that Spence had threatened to harm her if she told authorities anything.

Stilwell

While Wyatt and his posse, which included Holliday and his brother Warren, continued its search for Morgan's killers, Sheriff Behan put together his own posse to search for Earp, now wanted for Stilwell's murder. Just before conducting his infamous month long "vendetta ride", Wyatt had a famous confrontation with Behan, who sought to meet with him, warning the sheriff, "Johnny, if you're not careful you'll see me once too often."

Warren Earp

Before Behan could find him, the vendetta posse killed a cowboy named Florentino Cruz, also known as Indian Charlie, based on a rumor that he was involved in killing Morgan. Soon thereafter, the posse killed Curley Bill Brocius, Wyatt's nemesis from a few years earlier, though there was no evidence that Bronchus was involved with Morgan's death. The lawless vendetta to avenge the killing of Morgan quickly erased any support he may have had from the residents or businesses of Tombstone.

By the time the Earp Vendetta Ride was over, the posse had killed four outlaws. On April 13, 1882, Earp and Sadie Marcus left Arizona and went to Gunnison, Colorado to weather the storm. Mattie had already left for California and was with Virgil and his family. Wyatt expected the same businessmen who had financed him on his "Vendetta Ride" to come through and work out a pardon for the crimes he had committed so he could return to Tombstone and run for sheriff. But by this time many in Tombstone were glad to have him gone, and after six months of waiting it was apparent that a pardon would never come. Earp and his new common-law wife, who would remain with him for the rest of his life, went west again and headed to San Francisco.

Wanted for murder and with little, if any, support from the town, it was time for Earp and Holliday to leave Arizona in Spring 1882. It was also time for the friends to part ways. Mattie Earp was already in California with Virgil, where she would wait in vain for Wyatt to return. He may not have become sheriff, but he did get Behan's woman, and Sadie Marcus would remain with Wyatt for the rest of his life. Earp and his new common-law wife headed to San Francisco, while Doc Holliday stayed in Colorado.

Chapter 5: Holliday's Final Years

Holliday could not have returned to Arizona if he wanted to, at least not without facing a possible death sentence, but when he arrived in Denver in May 1882, he was arrested for Stilwell's murder. Behan made it clear that if Holliday appeared back in Tombstone, he would see to it that Holliday hanged and called for his extradition back to Arizona. With some intervention from Wyatt, who called on his old friend and the sheriff of Trinidad, Colorado, Bat Masterson, the extradition was blocked. Masterson had pulled some political strings, which evidently went as high as the governor's office.

The seminal moments associated with Holliday were now behind him, but Holliday's final years were marked by much of the same events as the prior 15 years of his life. He followed the gambling circuit around Colorado as his health permitted, never quite able to escape his reputation or bloodshed. Holliday and Wyatt were falsely accused of killing the cowboy Johnny Ringo, a friend of Ike Clanton's and Frank Stilwell's, in Arizona, though neither men were anywhere near the state at the time. It's possible that Doc was implicated simply because of the bad blood that previously existed between him and Ringo. In Tombstone in January 1882, only 3 months after the Shootout at the O.K. Corral, Holliday got into a heated argument with Ringo and allegedly said, "All I want of you is ten paces out in the street." A duel was stopped only by Tombstone's police, who arrested both of them.

Ringo

Though Doc almost certainly had nothing to do with Ringo's murder, Doc did indeed shoot Billy Allen in the arm over a $5 debt in 1884. This case actually went to trial, but on March 28, 1885, the jury believed that Doc had acted in self-defense, even if there was little evidence to support this.

The altitude of Colorado was not good for a man with consumption, and any gains he made in his battle against the disease in New Mexico and Arizona were soon wiped away in the Rocky Mountains. With his hair now gray, his body wasting away, and a growing dependence on alcohol to ease his misery, Holliday had a reunion with Earp in a hotel lobby in Denver in May 1885. Sadie watched the meeting from across the room, and both she and Wyatt were shocked at Holliday's appearance. When they parted, there were tears in Wyatt's eyes. Later in Denver, Holliday also ran into his old nemesis, Milt Joyce, but by the point in his life, Doc was not looking for trouble and left Joyce alone.

In May 1887, Holliday took a train to Glenwood Springs, Colorado. Glenwood Springs not only had gambling halls, it had waters that he hoped would help him the way the springs of New Mexico had. Unfortunately, they did not, and Doc's health deteriorated rapidly. In September, he developed pneumonia, from which he never recovered.

Naturally, Holliday's death has been the subject of controversy and speculation. On the morning of November 8, 1887, John Henry Holliday died at the Glenwood Hotel at the age of 36. Legend had it that as he lay dying, Holliday looked at his feet, presumably amused that he was dying with his boots off. For one of the West's most notorious gunslingers, Holliday and countless others probably assumed that he would "die with his boots on" in a gunfight. According to this legend, the nurses said that his last words were, "Damn, this is funny." Given his illness, however, modern historians believe Holliday would've been incapable of speaking coherently in his final days. It was also widely believed that Wyatt was there when Doc died, but Wyatt would not hear about his death for months. And even though Kate later claimed to have been there, most accounts say Holliday was alone when he died.

Given the course of Doc's life and death, perhaps it's not surprising that there is some speculation over his final resting place. It was believed that Doc was buried in Linwood Cemetery overlooking Glenwood Springs, but since it was November the frozen ground may have made it difficult for Holliday to actually be buried there, since it was was only accessible via a difficult mountain road. Holliday's biographer, Gary Roberts, has noted that other bodies were definitely transported to the Linwood Cemetery in November 1887, and that newspapers of the time stated Doc was buried there.

Even if Doc was buried there, the exact placement of his body was lost over time, leading the cemetery to erect a headstone in a random location on the grounds. However, the cemetery's initial headstone incorrectly listed the year of his birth as 1852 instead of 1851. Thus, it was eventually replaced by a more accurate headstone.

Chapter 6: The Doc Holliday Legend

Like other men of the Western frontier, especially his friend Wyatt Earp, Doc Holliday was as much myth as man after his death. At least part of his story has been depicted in film, including "My Darling Clementine" in 1936, "Gunfight at the OK Corral" in 1957, and "Tombstone" in 1993. Stacy Keach played him in the first movie to feature him as the main character in "Doc" in 1971. In 2011, Mary Doria Russell published the critically acclaimed novel, "Doc," a work of historical fiction that has been hailed by critics for shining new light on the man that everyone thought they already knew. Later that year, HBO announced that Doc would be getting his own television series, based on Russell's novel.

Doc Holliday did not lead the life that seemed to be his destiny. John Henry Holliday was an educated, handsome, and witty man could have been a dentist and a member of high society in the South. Instead, circumstances both within his control and outside of his control conspired to create Doc Holliday, who spent his adult life under the dark image of a cold-blooded killer in the West, a reputation that was unquestionably partly his own creation. In one interview with a newspaper, after being asked if his conscience ever troubled him, Holliday reportedly answered, "I coughed that up with my lungs years ago."

Holliday left behind no documents, no records, and no children to tell his story, leaving historians to piece together the life of a boy who grew up during the Reconstruction Era in the South and became an icon of the West. This has left much open to interpretation, making an accurate profile of his life extremely challenging. Virgil Earp himself may have summed it up best in an 1882 interview with the Arizona Daily Star, explaining, "There was something very peculiar about Doc. He was gentlemanly, a good dentist, a friendly man, and yet outside of us boys I don't think he had a friend in the Territory. Tales were told that he had murdered men in different parts of the country; that he had robbed and committed all manner of crimes, and yet when persons were asked how they knew it, they could only admit that it was hearsay, and that nothing of the kind could really be traced up to Doc's account."

Regardless of which Holliday stories are true or embellished legend, what is clear is that Holliday had no great achievements that might set him apart from other men of the 19th century. And yet he has become a household name, second perhaps only to Wyatt Earp among the legends of the West. Why is there so much interest in a man that many believe was a hotheaded gunman at best and a killer at worst, even if neither are completely accurate descriptions him? Perhaps it is in the empathy for the boy that lost his mother to the same dreaded disease that would kill him. Perhaps it is a measure of understanding for a man who could not have his one true love because she happened to be his cousin. Perhaps it is simply because the idea of a dentist running with the likes of Wyatt Earp is too good of a story to pass up. Whatever the reasons, Holliday the man will certainly continue to be obscured by Holliday the legend, which has made him an indelible figure of the West.

Bibliography

"Bat Masterson Not Impressed by Doc Holliday." *Territorial News.* December 15, 2010.

Bell, Bob Boze. *The Illustrated Life and Times of Doc Holliday.* Phoenix: Tri-Star Boze Publications, 1994.

Guinn, Jeff. *The Last Gunfight.* New York: Simon & Schuster. 2011.

Roberts, Gary L. *Doc Holliday: The Life and Legend.* Hoboken, New Jersey: Wiley & Sons. 2006.

Turner, Alfred, ed. *The O.K. Corral Inquest.* College Station, Texas: Creative Publishing Company, 1981.

Made in the USA
Middletown, DE
10 November 2024